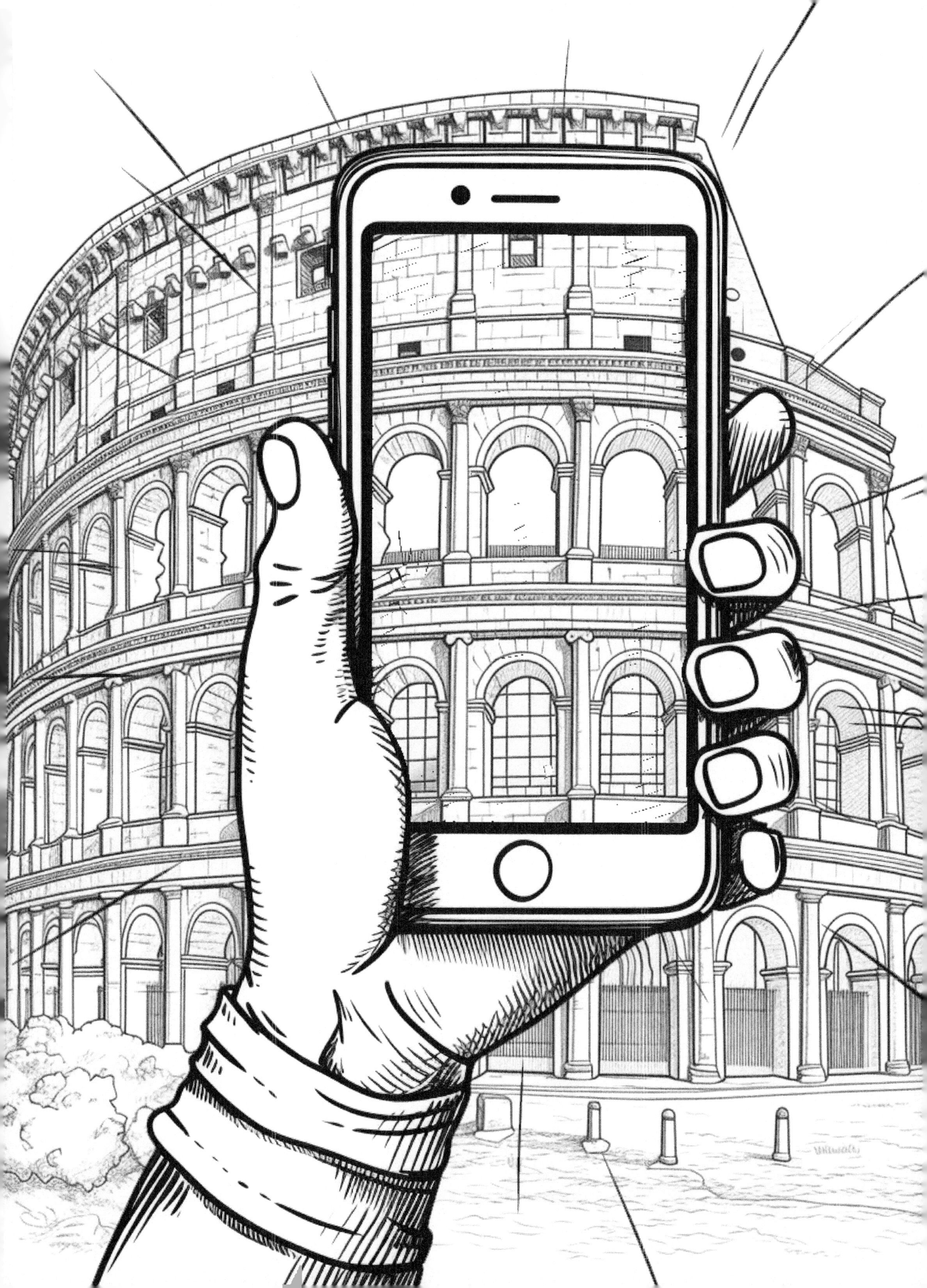

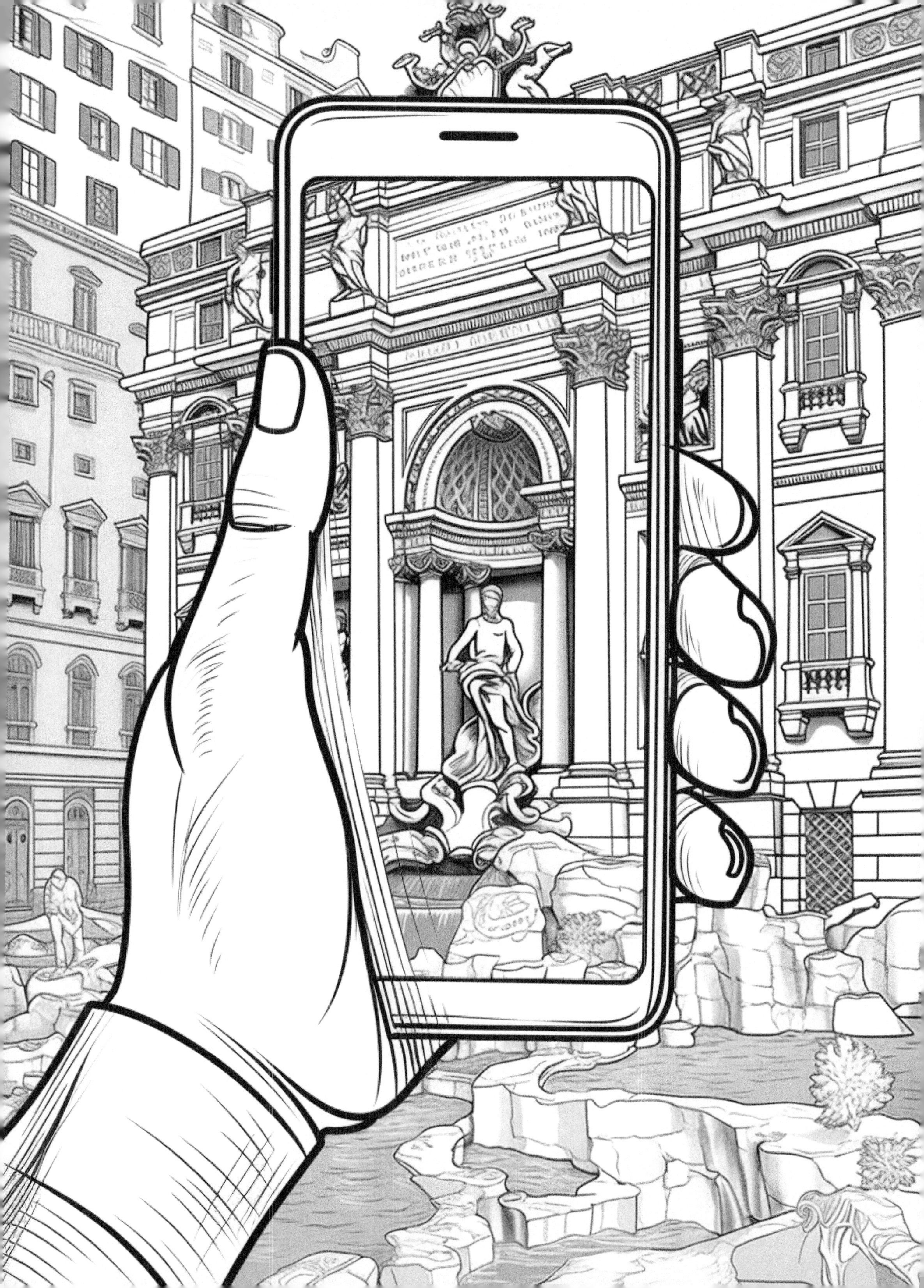

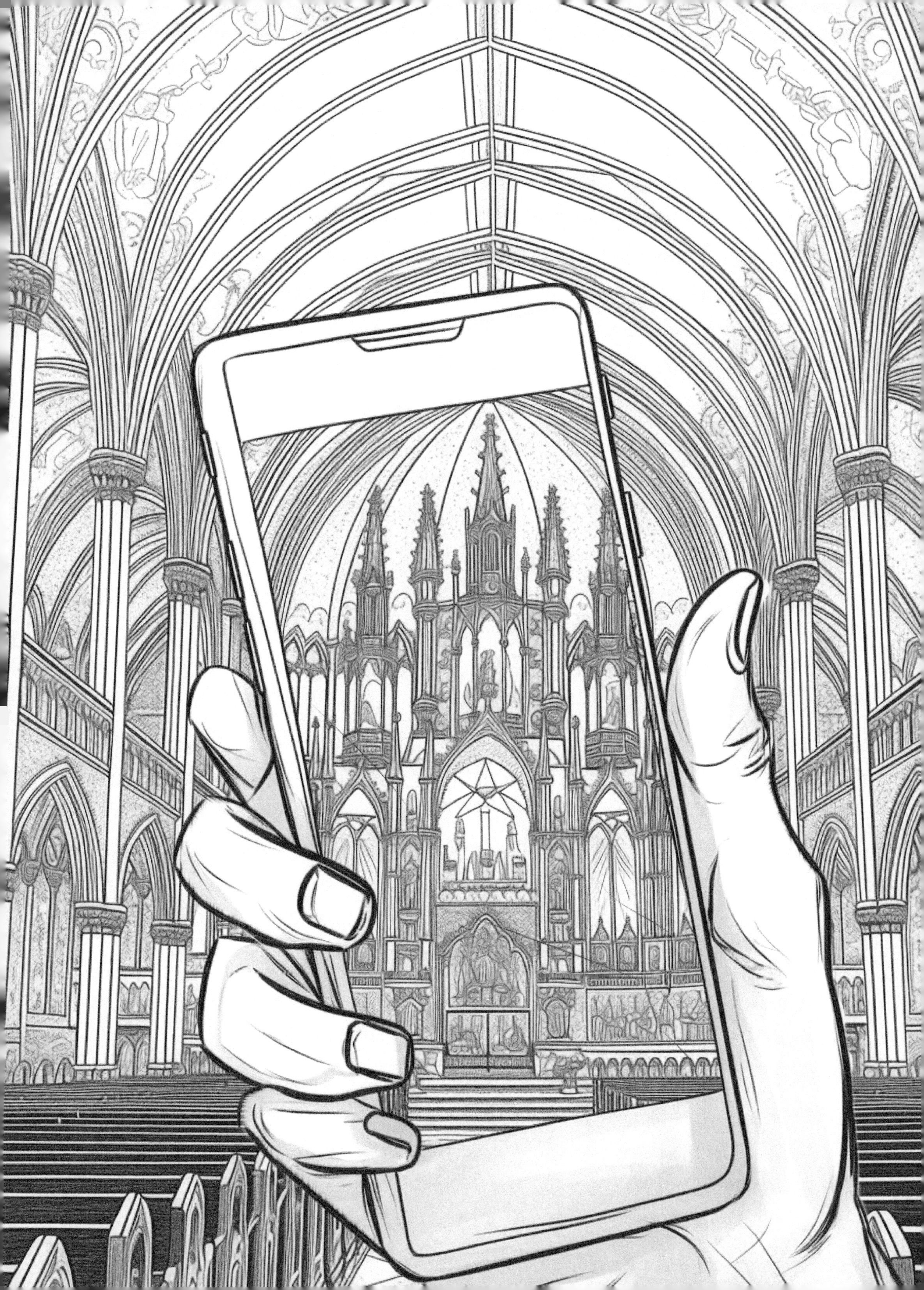

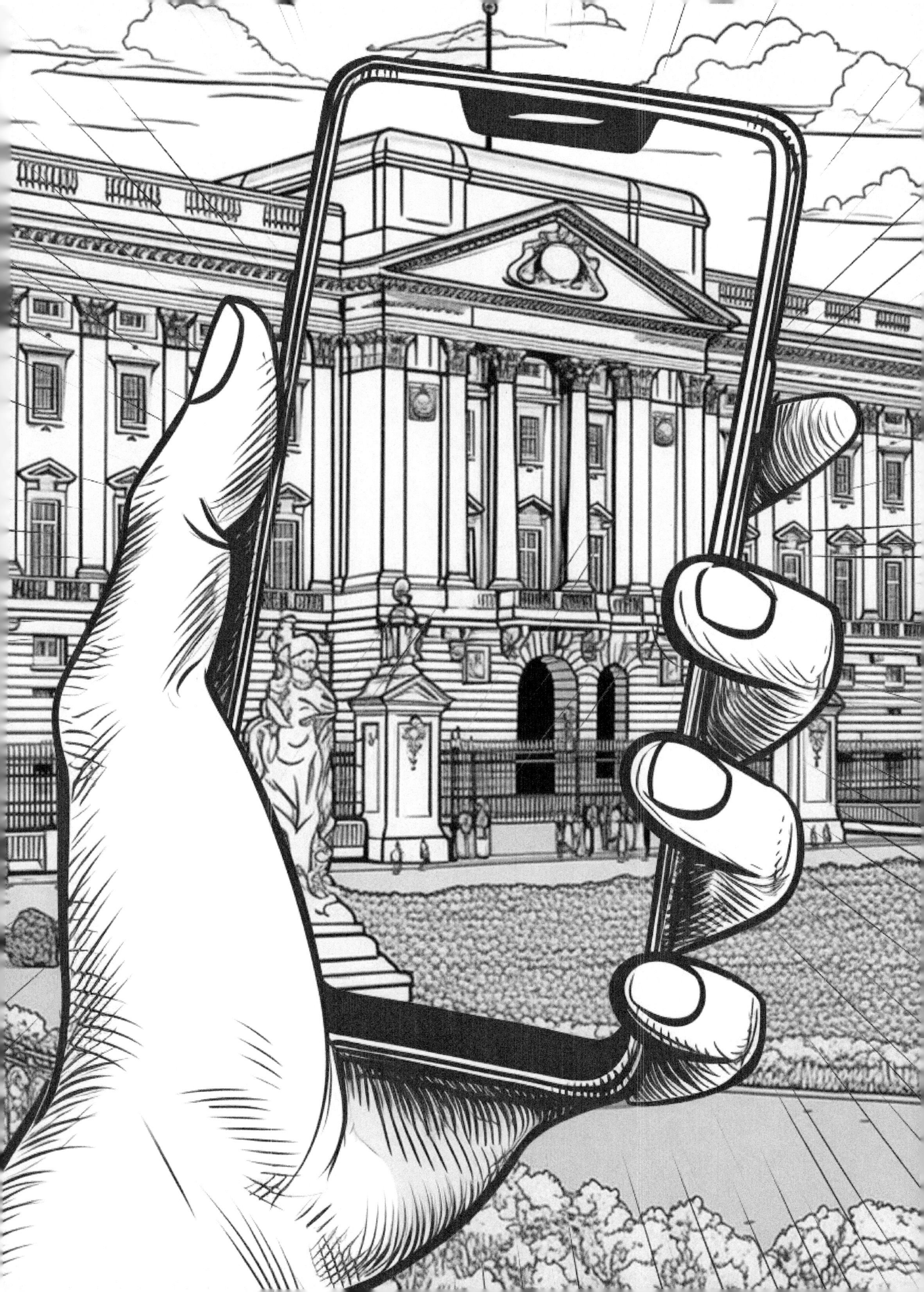

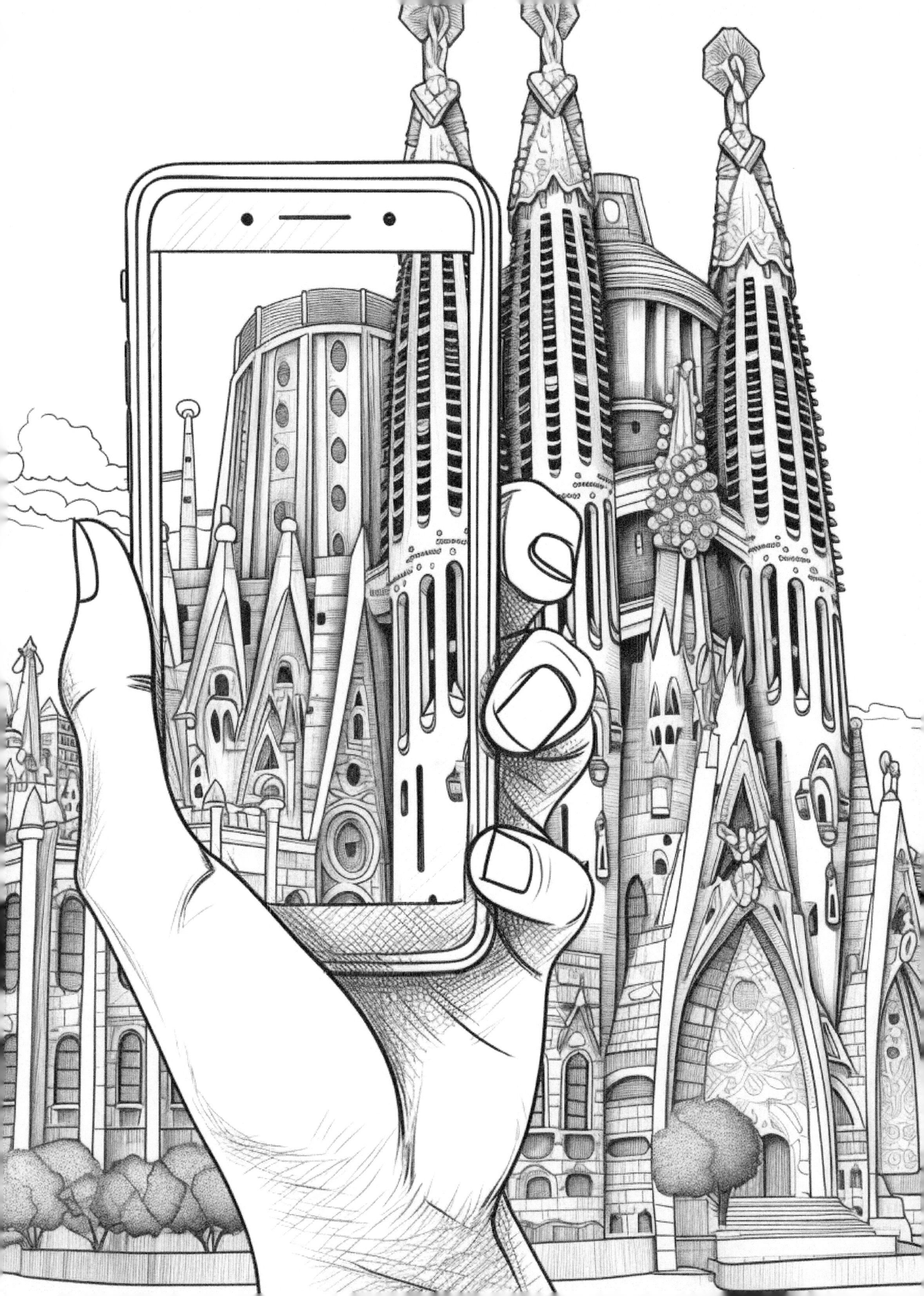

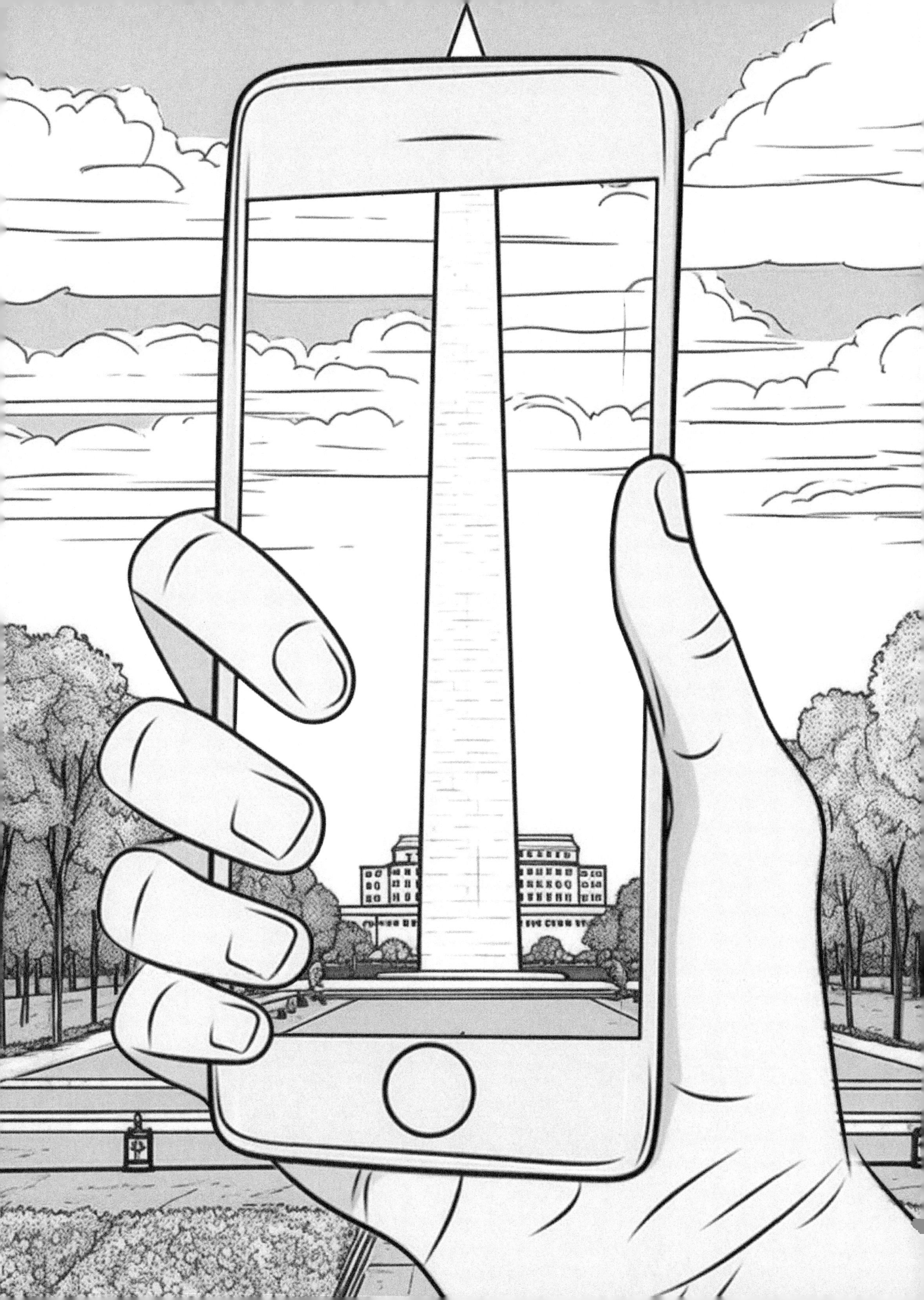

WME
ONNI
DEK

Printed in Great Britain
by Amazon

42761253R00046